Beginners

By Tim Crouch

Beginners was first performed at the Unicorn Theatre, London, on Wednesday 28 March 2018 with the following cast:

Cast
Lucy/Jenny – Pandora Colin
Bart/Adrian – Rob Das
Nigel/Steve – Neil D'Souza
Joy/Maddie – Jacqui Dubois
Sandy – Amalia Vitale

Child Bart – Rowan Davies-Moore / Archie MacGregor
Child Joy – Nekisha Eric / Atinuke Akinrinade
Child Lucy – Ella Scott / Emilija Trajkovic
Child Nigel – Ethan Dattani / Milan Verma

Director	Tim Crouch
Set & Costume Design	Chloe Lamford
	& Camilla Clarke
Composer	Nick Powell
Lighting Design	Zoe Spurr
Associate Director (Children)	Cath Greenwood
Assistant Director	Tom McClane
Movement Consultant	Janine Fletcher
Stage Manager	Hannah Moore
Deputy Stage Manager	Sarah Barnes
Assistant Stage Manager	Beth Absalom
Wardrobe Supervisor	Cristiano Casimiro
Chaperone	Elaine Henderson-Boyle

BIOGRAPHIES

Pandora Colin (Lucy)

Theatre includes: *Julius Caesar, The Country Wife* (Sheffield Crucible); *The Vote* (Donmar Warehouse); *Cornelius* (59E59 Theatres, Brits Off Broadway); *The Dark Earth and the Light Sky, House Of Bernada Alba* (Almeida Theatre); *Stephen and the Sexy Partridge* (Trafalgar Studios); *Sixty-Six Books, If There Is I Haven't Found It Yet* (Bush Theatre); *After The Dance, Every Good Boy Deserves Favour, some trace of her..., Women of Troy* (National Theatre); *Serious Money* (Birmingham Rep); *Kindertransport* (Hampstead Theatre/Tour); *You Might As Well Live* (Pleasance, Edinburgh Festival/New End Theatre); *Much Ado About Nothing* (Salisbury Playhouse); *Design for Living* (Bath Theatre Royal); *Man of Mode* (Exeter Northcott Theatre); *Mariana Pineda* (Arcola Theatre).

Television includes: *Line of Duty, Count Arthur Strong, Delicious* (seasons 1 & 2), *Toast of London, Penny Dreadful, Mr Selfridge, Titanic, Hotel Babylon, Life Begins, Coupling, Doctors, Ny-Lon, Black Books, Watermelon, The Pooters, Extremely Dangerous, The Dark Room, Close Relations, The Peter Principal, Wycliff, Tears Before Bedtime, In Your Dreams.*

Film includes: *Film Stars Don't Die In Liverpool, The Lady In The Van, I Give It A Year, A Bunch of Amateurs, Run Fat Boy, Run.*

Radio includes: *The Amateur Marriage, The Art of Deception, Summer Crossing, The Happiness Foundation* (BBC Radio 4).

Rob Das (Bart)

After graduating as an actor from the Amsterdam School of Arts in 1995, Rob Das started his career at Het Zuidelijk Toneel (Tilburg, Netherlands) under then Artistic Director Ivo van Hove who directed Rob in *Splendid's, Faces, The Unloved, Romeo and Juliet.*

Rob has worked extensively for Dutch television and cinema, and has performed in the American mini-series about the life of Anne Frank and, more recently, performed in *ANNE,* a new stage adaptation of Anne Frank's diaries at Theater Amsterdam.

He has completed a Masters at the Binger Film Institute, and works as an editor, writer and director alongside his acting career.

Neil D'Souza (Nigel)

Neil trained at RADA. Theatre includes: *The Hypocrite* (Royal Shakespeare Company); *Coming Up* (Watford Palace); *How To Hold Your Breath, Khandan* (Royal Court); *Drawing the Line* (Hampstead Theatre); *Much Ado About Nothing, Midnight's Children* (Royal Shakespeare Company); *Tintin* (West End); *The Man of Mode* (National Theatre); *Twelfth Night* (West End); *A Midsummer Night's Dream* (Mercury Theatre Colchester); *The Merchant of Venice, The Honest Whore* (Shakespeare's Globe).

Television includes: *Eastenders, Hustle, Citizen Khan, Doctors, Happiness, Undercover, Holby City, Don't Take My Baby, Back Up* (BBC); *Humans, Not Safe For Work, Friday Night Dinner* (Channel 4); *In The Long Run* (Sky); *Amerikan Kannibal* (Discovery).

Film includes: *Filth, Still Life, Closed Circuit, Wild Target, Another Me, My Sweet Home, Italian Movies.*

Radio includes: *The Red Oleander, Goan Flame, Ask Mina, Recent Events at Collington House* (BBC Radio 4).

Neil is also a writer whose plays include: *Coming Up* (Watford Palace); *Small Miracle* (Tricycle Theatre); *Five Beats to the Bar* (BBC Radio 4); Westway (BBC World Service).

Jacqui Dubois (Joy)

Theatre includes: *People Places and Things* (National Theatre/West End/USA), *Fela!* (National Theatre/USA), *Emil and the Detectives* (National Theatre). West End theatre includes: *The Lion King, Rent, The Harder They Come* (and US Tour), *Fame, The Full Monty, Sophisticated Ladies, All You Need Is Love, Children of Eden.*

Other credits include: Kate Bush's *Before the Dawn* (Hammersmith Apollo), *Ghost!* (UK Tour), *Carousel* (Chichester Festival Theatre), *The Amen Corner, Blues In The Night, Little Shop of Horrors, Mary Stuart, Rehab: The Musical, The Realness, Looking For Obama, The Wizard of Oz, Anansi Steals The Wind, Dr Livingstone I Presume, JFK, Sweet Lorraine, The Boys From Syracuse, The Cabaret of Dr Caligari, Peacemaker.*

Television and film includes: *Hedda, Bye Bye Inkhead, Pigsty.* Radio includes: *The Tokolosh.*

As a vocalist Jaqui has worked with various artists including: Kate Bush, Nomad, Puff Daddy, Latoya Jackson, T.S.O.S.F, Jam & Spoon, Bass X, Dance to Trance, Digital Orgasm.

Amalia Vitale (Sandy)

Amalia trained at the Birmingham School of Acting. Theatre includes: *The Lion the Witch and the Wardrobe* (West Yorkshire Playhouse); *Jeramee, Hartleby, Ooooglemore* (Unicorn Theatre); *Primetime* (Royal Court); *Beauty and the Beast* (Cambridge Junction); *The Light Princess* (Tobacco Factory); *Hysteria* (Theatre Royal Bath); *Aloe Aloe* (Arcola Theatre); *In A Box* (Off Cut Festival); *The Toy Theatre* (Birmingham REP); *Hunting of the Snark* (Latitude Festival).

Television includes: *Midsomer Murders*, *Endeavour* (ITV), *Casualty* (BBC).

Amalia co-runs All in theatre. Their plays include *Love Sick*, *Civilised* and *Bon Ami*. allintheatre.com

Tim Crouch – Writer & Director

Tim was an actor for many years before starting to write – and he still performs in much of his work.

His plays include: *My Arm*, *ENGLAND* (a play for galleries), the OBIE award-winning *An Oak Tree*, *The Author*, *Adler & Gibb* and (with Andy Smith) *what happens to the hope at the end of the evening*. Tim tours his work nationally and internationally. He also writes for younger audiences. A series of plays inspired by Shakespeare's lesser characters includes *I, Malvolio* and *I, Peaseblossom*. For the RSC, Tim has directed *The Taming of the Shrew*, *King Lear* and *I, Cinna (the poet)* – all for young audiences. Other directing credits include *Jeramee, Hartleby and Ooooglemore* for the Unicorn Theatre and *The Complete Deaths* for Spymonkey.

Tim is published by Oberon Books. timcrouchtheatre.co.uk @timcrouch1964

Chloe Lamford – Set & Costume Designer

Chloe trained at the Wimbledon School of Art. In 2013 she won the Arts Foundation Fellowship Award for Design for Performance: Set & Costume. Chloe is an associate artist at the Royal Court Theatre and a resident of Somerset House Studios.

Theatre includes: *John* (National Theatre); *Gun Dog* (Royal Court); *Show Room* (installation created for Somerset House); *Jubilee* (Lyric Hammersmith); *Mens* (visual direction for singer Wende Snijders); *Atmen* and *Ophelias Zimmer* (Schaubühne, Berlin); *De Maiden* (Toneelgroep, Amsterdam); *Amadeus*, *Rules for Living*, *The World of Extreme Happiness* (National Theatre); *1984* (Broadway, West End/Headlong/Almeida); *Our Ladies* of *Perpetual Succour* (West End/National Theatre/National Theatre Scotland); *Victory Condition, B , Road, Unreachable, The Twits, God Bless The Child, How to Hold Your Breath, Circle Mirror Transformation, Teh Internet is Serious Business, 2071, Open Court* (Royal Court); *The Hamilton Complex* (Hetpaleis/Unicorn Theatre/LIFT); *The Tempest* (Donmar at King's Cross); *The Events* (ATC/Young Vic); *Disco Pigs, Sus,* costume design for *Blackta* (Young Vic); *My Shrinking Life, Appointment with the Wicker Man, Knives in Hens* (National Theatre Scotland); *Praxis Makes Perfect, The Radicalisation of Bradley Manning* (National Theatre Wales); *Boys* (Headlong Theatre); *Cannibals, The Gate Keeper* (Manchester Royal Exchange).

Camilla Clarke – Set & Costume Designer

Camilla trained at the Royal Welsh College of Music and Drama. In 2014 she won the Lord Williams Memorial Prize for Design, and in 2015 she won the Linbury Prize for Stage Design.

Theatre includes: *Elephant* (Birmingham REP); *Bad Roads* (Royal Court); *Frogman* (Curious Detective/Traverse Theatre); *The Day After, Trial By Jury* (ENO); *No Place For A Woman* (Theatre 503); *Wind Resistance* (Royal Lyceum Theatre); *Wish You Were Here!* co-designed with Chloe Lamford (Somerset House); *Human Animals* (Royal Court); *Much Ado About Nothing* (Mercury Theatre Colchester); *Yuri* (Chapter Arts Centre); *Segulls* (Volcano Theatre); *Triptych* (Wales Millennium Centre); *The Wonderful World of Dissocia* (RWCMD), *Don Quixote* (Elan Frantoio, Italy).

Nick Powell – Composer

Nick is a composer and sound designer. Theatre includes: *Julius Caesar* (The Bridge Theatre); *Peter Pan* (Regent's Park Open Air Theatre); *The Ferryman, The Nether* (Royal Court/West End); *City of Glass* (59 Productions/Lyric Hammersmith); *Cold Calling: The Artic Project* (Birmingham Rep/CBSO); *The Inn at Lydda* (RSC); *Unreachable, X* (Royal Court); *Lord of the Flies* (UK Tour); *Lanark: A Life in Three Acts* (Citizens Theatre/Edinburgh International Festival); sound design for *Wolf Hall, Bring Up The Bodies* (RSC/West End/Broadway); *Dunsinane* (National Theatre of Scotland/RSC/UK/US Tours); *Of Mice and Men* (Birmingham Rep/Tour); *Othello* (National Theatre); *A Life of Galileo, Richard III, The Drunks, God in Ruins* (RSC).

Nick also writes extensively for TV & film. He is one half of OSKAR who have released two albums and produced installations for the V&A and CCA, as well as written live soundtracks for Prada in Milan. In 2017, Nick was composer for 59 Productions' *Bloom*, opening event of the Edinburgh

Festival and *Reflections* – the 20th anniversary celebration of the Guggenheim Museum in Bilbao.

Zoe Spurr – Lighting Designer

Zoe trained at the Royal Central School of Speech and Drama. Theatre includes: *Elephant* (Birmingham REP); *Collective Rage* (Southwark Playhouse); *Tiny Dynamite* (Old Red Lion Theatre); *Phoenix Rising* with Big House Theatre, *Elton John's Glasses* (Watford Palace Theatre); *The Magic Flute* with Opera Up Close (Soho Theatre/UK Tour); *The Scar Test* (Untold Arts/Soho Theatre); *Skate Hard Turn Left* (BAC); *The Drive* (Angel Exit/UK Tour), *The North! The North!* (UK Tour); *Natives* (Boundless Theatre/Southwark Playhouse); *Hidden* (UK Tour); *Good Dog* with Tiata Fahodzi (Watford Palace Theatre/UK Tour); *The Truth* (Central Szinhaz, Budapest); *Muted* (Bunker Theatre); *Erwartung/Twice Through The Heart* (Shadwell Opera/Hackney Showroom); *The Knife of Dawn* (Roundhouse); *Affection* (Outbox Theatre site specific at The Glory).

zoespurrlighting.co.uk

Cath Greenwood – Associate Director (Children)

Cath is the learning associate at the Unicorn Theatre and has been in post since 2007. Her primary role is to connect teachers and pupils with the artistic programme through practical drama activities that enrich and extend their visit.

With many years' experience working across theatre and drama education, Cath has worked in schools, pupil referral units, hospitals, prisons and care homes, as well as for a number of theatres including: The Cockpit Theatre, Northampton TIE, Theatre Powys, Theatre Company Blah Blah Blah, Theatre Clwyd, Magic Me.

Tom McClane – Assistant Director

Tom McClane trained as an actor at Drama Centre London and went on to complete an MFA in directing at Birkbeck.

Directing includes: *Hedda Gabler, Ghosts, A Doll's House* (Guildford School of Acting); *Twelfth Night* (Birmingham School of Acting).

He has recently reassembled *A Woman Before a Glass* (Jermyn Street Theatre) directed in New York by Austin Pendleton. He has also assisted directors Bijan Sheibani, Lotte Wakeman and Alice Hamilton.

THE UK'S THEATRE FOR YOUNG AUDIENCES

For the Unicorn Theatre

The Unicorn is the UK's leading theatre for young audiences, producing an eclectic and surprising programme of work year-round for children aged 6 months to 18 years. Based in a purpose-built home at London Bridge, they aim to connect artists and audiences through a broad range of work that is honest, refreshing and international in outlook, across a range of disciplines.

Artistic Director Purni Morell
Executive Director Anneliese Davidsen
Producer Niamh Dilworth
Learning Associate Cath Greenwood
Finance Director Julie Renwick
Finance Officer Hattie Davis
Community Projects Director Sally Pembroke
General Manager Amy Smith
Stage Door Keepers Emma Berensten, Paul Brewster, John Cockerill, Oliver Gatz, Nadia Giscir, Jessica Hayles, Anna Johnson, Emma Thomson, Clare Quinn and Gary Sheldrake

Technical Director Matt Ledbury
Production Manager Jennifer Taillefer
Company Stage Manager Sarah Julie Pujol
Building Maintenance Manager Adam Pearson
Production Coordinator Liz Lawson
Production Coordinator Maternity Cover Andrew Pellett
Senior Technician Rob Johnson
Technicians Kevin Bolt, Holly Curtis, Alfie Leigh

Director of Development Tamzin Golding
Development Associate Rebecca Kendall
Development Manager (Trusts and Foundations) Chloe Booth
Development Administrator Zoe Bennett

Director of Marketing and Communications Helen Tovey
Events Producer Sair Smith
Schools Relationship Manager Ella MacFadyen
Schools Relationship Officer Yasmin Joseph
Lead Drama Practitioner Lucy Dear
Press and PR (freelance) Clióna Roberts, CRPR
Marketing Manager Jane Dodson
Marketing Officer Jessica Young
Box Office Manager Mal Chudzinska
Box Office Supervisor Rhys Evans
Deputy Front of House Manager Elisabeth Fowler

Performance Managers Joseph Winer, Alice Sillett

Front of House Staff Daisy Adams, Jessica Brodie, Jackie Downer, Dwaynica Greaves, Ellie Goffe, Georgia Hardcastle, Housni Hassan, Josephine Jobbins, Ellie Jones, Sarah King, Daniel Knott, Hannah Margerison, Amy Millward, Carole Mitchell, Thea Medland, Cecilia Morgan, Matthew Newell, Damien Noyce, Robert Pearce, Henry Reynolds, Emma Russell, Paula Shaw, Gary Sheldrake, Malinda Smith, Isobel Tyrrell and Alicia Walker

Box Office Assistants Chantelle Burley, James Chamberlain, Samara Gannon, Frey Kwa Hawking and Tiffany Murphy

Board of Directors John Langley (Chair), Anneliese Davidsen, Simon Davidson, Henny Finch, Giles Havergal CBE, Purni Morell, Agnes Quashie, Colin Simon and Sarah West

Ambassadors HRH The Duchess of Cornwall (Patron), Juliet Stevenson (President), Quentin Blake, Joanna David, Dame Judi Dench, Mel Giedroyc, Mishal Husain, Jude Law, Michael Morpurgo, Philip Pullman and Meera Syal

unicorntheatre.com | 020 7645 0560 | 147 Tooley Street, SE1 2HZ
Registered charity no: 225751 & 1087149

We would like to thank:
The Mackintosh Foundation
Molecule Theatre
The Royal Victoria Hall Foundation
The Sylvia Waddilove Foundation

Deborah Mingham of Entify for making the props
Nine Leaves Knitters (@nineleavesknitters) for knitting the hats
Hans Kemna Casting, Netherlands
The Rigging Team for providing us with their specialist rigging services
Chauvet Lighting for providing the lighting fixtures

The parents and schools of our young cast: Esther Akinrinade, Sophie Cameron, Dipika Dattani, Rachel Davies, Diana MacGregor, Margaret Mugi, Blagoje and Daliborka Trajkovic, Anisha and Dean Verma. Charles Dickens Primary School, City of London School, Goodrich Community Primary School, Hazelwood School, Kennington Park Academy, Kew College and Wallands Community Primary School.

The Unicorn Theatre is an NPO organisation and is grateful to Arts Council England for their continued support of the Unicorn Theatre.

Supported using public funding by
**ARTS COUNCIL
ENGLAND**

BEGINNERS

Tim Crouch

BEGINNERS

OBERON BOOKS
LONDON
WWW.OBERONBOOKS.COM

First published in 2018 by Oberon Books Ltd
521 Caledonian Road, London N7 9RH
Tel: +44 (0) 20 7607 3637 / Fax: +44 (0) 20 7607 3629
e-mail: info@oberonbooks.com
www.oberonbooks.com

A catalogue record for this book is available from the British Library.

PB ISBN: 9781786823519
E ISBN: 9781786823526

Cover design by Julia Crouch

Printed on FSC accredited paper

Thanks

Hannah Ringham. Nigel Barratt. Joy Richardson. George Lasha. Ashley McGuire. Robby Cleiren. Bryony Hannah. Naomi Wirthner. Asma Yousfi, Giulia Lesa, Esteban Cardona Tenorio and Malachy Okorode. Purni Morell and all the staff of the Unicorn Theatre. Ed O'Brien and Radiohead. John Retallack. Hilary Stockill and the Nine Leaves Knitters. Nel Crouch and Rob Stockill. Jules, Joe and Owen.

Characters

JOY

SANDY

LUCY

BART

NIGEL

CHILD JOY

CHILD NIGEL

CHILD LUCY

CHILD BART

MADDIE

ADRIAN

JENNY

STEVE

Four beds.

The adult actors are all in their forties at least – except SANDY, who can be any adult age.

The performances of the adults are very 'adult'.

To start with, the children in this show are like the adults' daemons. They can be sensed but they can't properly be seen by the adult actors. They slowly take over the adult performances.

The sound of rain.

JOY is onstage as the audience enter.

Onstage is also a nine-year-old girl (CHILD JOY) who looks a bit like the actor playing JOY. She is wearing the child-like equivalent of what JOY is wearing. JOY and CHILD JOY do not connect with each other.

The sound of a car on a gravel drive. Car doors slamming.

JOY removes a realistic-looking gun from her jacket pocket. She listens.

CHILD JOY leaves.

In one swift move JOY hides behind her bed – visible to the audience, invisible to everyone else.

SANDY enters. Followed by LUCY with a pram and a suitcase.

LUCY gets out her phone and looks at it. Tension. Rain.

LUCY: (*Calling off.*) Jen. JEN.
        What's the password?
        The wifi, Jen, the INTERNET.

SANDY looks at LUCY.

        What is it?

SANDY goes towards where JOY is hiding.

JOY and the SANDY look at each other.

Sandy?

JOY puts her fingers to her lips.

SANDY steps up onto one of the beds.

Get here. HERE.

SANDY returns to LUCY. LUCY hits SANDY hard. SANDY recoils in shock.

Now you listen to me, I swear to god. You
don't wake the baby and you don't fool
around. They'll throw you out, you hear me.
You want that, do you, outside? You want –
(Interrupted.)

(Calling off.) She's with me.

You do it. I'm busy. YOU DO IT. *(To
SANDY.)* See what I mean?

(Calling off.) The backpack on the – in the
Volvo. The VOLVO.

To SANDY.

Come here.

SANDY goes to LUCY. LUCY hugs her. The hug becomes threatening.

To your place, now. NOW.

SANDY goes to the control desk at the side of the stage. LUCY checks on her baby.

It's alright now, petal, you're here now.
Weren't you good in the car, weren't you?
You sleep on, sleep, darling, mummy's –

A backpack drops from the sky.

(Calling off.) HEY. Don't just throw it
in. Don't just – KEEP YOUR VOICE
DOWN, ANYWAY, SHE'S ASLEEP,
SHE'S SLEEPING.

LUCY picks up the backpack. Takes out an individual Ribena carton. Drinks it in one.

> Hello, old place. You missed me?
>
> Draw these curtains. Get some air in. Isn't that right, Sandy?

SANDY presses a button. Black out. Rain.

Lights up.

BART is there, in a raincoat. He's carrying a case and a holdall.

LUCY: I always have by the window.

BART: How about here?

LUCY: That's Nigel's.

BART points at another bed.

> Joy's.

BART takes off his coat and starts to unpack.

LUCY keeps an eye on him, like he's a dangerous but rather attractive animal. She attends to her phone throughout.

BART: They let you have a phone.

LUCY: I get what I want.

BART: How old is your baby?

LUCY: Six months.

BART: What's his name?

LUCY: Jasmine.

BART: Are you Lucy?

	I met Paul and Penny –
LUCY:	Jenny. / Paul and *Jenny*.
BART:	– in the kitchen.
LUCY:	Have they opened the wine?
BART:	Yes.
LUCY:	They don't muck about.
BART:	You want to go / up there?
LUCY:	We can't find any towels. They say they provide towels but we can't find any. Every year there's something. Last year the heating conked out. Paul was on the phone for hours. They gave us a discount. Don't know why we come here. It's meant to be ready by three, and it's – what is it? – four now and they still haven't brought the towels and there's no milk, there's meant to be milk in the fridge, it says there'll – Hey.

BART has sat on NIGEL's bed.

What did I tell you?

That's Nigel's.

(Calling off.) YES, JEN, YES.
HE'S IN HERE.
BECAUSE I AM BUSY LIKE I SAID.

SIAN'S BED. SIANY'S.

(To BART.) First year Sian's not come.

BART:	There was room in the car.

LUCY puts her feet in first position.

4

BART:	You call her Jen.
LUCY:	So?
BART:	She looks like someone's rubbed a balloon over her head.
LUCY:	She doesn't care about that. She has more important things to think about. She's an environmental entomologist. She studies insects. Bees mostly. She's obsessed with bees. She's written a book about them, I have it in my bag, you should read it. They're dying out and if there are no bees then we'll all starve to death. She always says, 'What on god's green earth is going on?' Jen is helping to save the world.
BART:	She's a superhero.
LUCY:	Too fat to be a superhero. She has diabetes. I said she should save *herself* first before she saves the world and not drink so much. They just drink and smoke. All of them. That's why they come here. Their idea of a holiday. Paul never normally smokes but because it's a holiday. It's / disgusting.
BART:	They think they look cool but really they're just / killing themselves.
LUCY:	Killing themselves.

LUCY does a demi-plié.

	I mean they're in their forties for Pete's sake.
BART:	We're all slowly dying anyway.

LUCY puts her phone away.

LUCY:	How long did it take you to get here?

5

BART: I don't know.

LUCY: Paul always does M4, M5, A30.

BART: We went through Honiton.

LUCY: Where's Nigel?

BART: Still in the car.

BART sees JOY hiding. BART and JOY look at each other.

LUCY: They say this place is haunted. Someone died here and they still walk around. I don't believe in ghosts. This used to be the stables. You can still smell the horse.

BART: Maybe it's a ghost horse.

        Jasmine is a good sleeper.

LUCY: Is your name Bart?

BART: Bartolomeüs. But everyone calls me Bart.

LUCY: Like *The Simpsons.*

        Where's that from?

BART: The Netherlands.

LUCY: Jenny said you were Dutch.

BART: Dutch is the Netherlands.

LUCY: How do you know English?

BART: My dad was half-English.

LUCY: She's got an eye for English men, your mum, hasn't she? Your dad, now Steve.

        What's that?

BART: A karaoke machine. I thought we / could –

LUCY:	Sian and I have known each other since the beginning.
BART:	Right.
LUCY:	That's Sian's bed.
BART:	You said.
LUCY:	Last year she got off her face and tried to climb up the curtains. She brought all this down – the rail, the plaster. They've fixed it since then. You can see where they fixed it. We lost our deposit. It was pretty wild even by Sian's standards. I'm surprised they let us back.
	Last year was wild.
BART:	She didn't want to come this year.
LUCY:	I know.
BART:	She's still / not –
LUCY:	We message.
BART:	She wanted to be with her mum.
LUCY:	Have you been here before?
BART:	No.
LUCY:	Have you ever even been to Cornwall before?
BART:	No.
LUCY:	This is where we always come.
BART:	Yes.
LUCY:	Every summer.

BART:	Yes.
LUCY:	All together.
BART:	Yes.
LUCY:	Until this year.
BART:	I'm sorry.
LUCY:	I don't know what Steve was thinking.
BART:	People split up.
LUCY:	Nigel's taken it really hard.
BART:	You think?
LUCY:	*(As she speaks she sort of half-dances.)* They were the perfect couple, Fran and Steve. You could see it happening last summer. They were at each other's throats. Steve was probably already being unfaithful, I reckon. That's why Sian destroyed the curtains. They found this place, Fran and Steve. This was their idea. They were all at college – with Paul and Jen and Maddie – all of them – and they came here one summer. And now we all come here. The same house. Every year since the year dot. And every year I say, 'why don't we go somewhere else?' Somewhere hot. 'The Canary Islands to see the canaries.' But this is what we do. We come here to the middle of nowhere. But then Fran and Steve split up and now Steve is with your – what's her name?
BART:	Liesbeth.
LUCY:	And it's been a big year for Maddie.
BART:	I / heard.

LUCY:	We thought she wouldn't make it, but she has and we have to be, you know, really kind to Joy because she's been through a lot.
BART:	Nigel / told me.
LUCY:	And Maddie was even ill last summer and everyone thought it was just the flu or glandular fever. I remember her swimming in the cove and there were these bruises and I said, 'where did you get those bruises from, Maddie?' and she couldn't remember. And everyone thought it was nothing. No one thought for a minute it was cancer. I hate cancer.
BART:	Everyone hates cancer.
LUCY:	They'll invent a cure.
BART:	I wish they'd hurry up.
LUCY:	Does Liesbeth smoke? How did she meet Steve?
BART:	At a conference.
LUCY:	When the cat's away the mice will play.
BART:	There aren't any canaries on the Canary Islands. No more than any island not called Canary.
LUCY:	Last year was mad.
BART:	I went with my dad years ago.
LUCY:	You'll be coming here from now on for ever and ever and ever and ever.
BART:	Are you a dancer?

LUCY:	A ballet dancer.
BART:	That must be an amazing life.
LUCY:	It's extremely hard work.
BART:	I imagine.
LUCY:	The training and everything.
BART:	And with a baby.
LUCY:	It's absolutely exhausting.
	Have you met Joy?
BART:	No.
LUCY:	She's a flipping weirdo. She was a weirdo in the first place and now, with Maddie's cancer, she's even more so.

More unpacking. BART sees SANDY.

BART:	And what's your name?
LUCY:	Sandy. She's in my bad books.
BART:	Hi, Sandy.
LUCY:	She's not really allowed to be here but they turn a blind eye.
BART:	Okay.
LUCY:	Would you like to give her a biscuit?
BART:	Sure.

LUCY gets a packet of biscuits out from under the pram and hands one to BART.

BART gives it to SANDY.

LUCY:	Say thank you, Sandy.

BART:	Wouldn't it be cool if she actually said 'thank you'. 'Thank you so much for this biscuit, Bartolomeüs!'
LUCY:	Jen says that even if she could speak we wouldn't understand what she was saying.
	You can have one yourself if you want.
BART:	We stopped at McDonald's.
LUCY:	You're joking.
BART:	Outside Exeter.
LUCY:	Fran would never have gone to McDonald's.
	Did your dad die?
BART:	I admit I quite like McDonald's. So does Steve. And Nigel.
LUCY:	Where is he?
BART:	My dad?
	Nowhere.
LUCY:	Nigel.
BART:	Asleep in the car. He's exhausted from the journey.
LUCY:	Nigel is a numpty.
BART:	Is that good?
LUCY:	It's like a big stupid idiot.
BART:	Do you think there's heaven?
LUCY:	You don't happen to know the wi-fi password do you by any chance?
BART:	I've just arrived.

LUCY:	Last year it was applecottage17, but that doesn't seem to work.
	Why does everything have to change?

BART takes a biscuit from LUCY. He lies down on his bed.

SANDY approaches.

LUCY:	No. No you don't. Back you go. Go on. Back.

SANDY returns to her control desk.

Don't look at me like that. Don't.

SANDY presses a button. Black out. Sound of rain.

Lights up.

NIGEL is in his doctor's coat with bag and stethoscope. He is carrying an umbrella. He doesn't see BART.

NIGEL:	I mean.
LUCY:	Nigel.
NIGEL:	Who in their right mind goes into Honiton on a bank holiday / weekend?
LUCY:	Nigel.
NIGEL:	And Liesbeth goes, 'Ooh, Schteve, let's go through the town. It will be pretty.' And we're already running late as it is and it's tipping down and the traffic is – and it's *Honiton*, for pity's sake, it's not the hanging gardens of Babylon. And there's a market on or something, so the traffic is – But 'Schteve' is like putty in her hands. So we park up and

they get out so she can buy some fudge or
something –

LUCY: Nigel.

NIGEL: – and they actually kissed. That's the point
of what I'm saying to you. They kissed. In
the shop. He didn't think I could see from
the car but I could and I'm like 'Get a room.'
And Bart is oblivious to it all. Have you met
him yet, / Bart?

LUCY: Nigel.

NIGEL: He thinks we're like brothers or something
now that we live in the same house and we
had to listen to his heavy metal the whole
journey. And I wanted to listen to *Wicked*
but they wouldn't let me. And I should
have stayed with Siany. And this is *our* place
where *we* go and –

LUCY: NIGEL.

NIGEL sees BART.

NIGEL: I hear Jasmine's not been too well.

LUCY: She's asleep.

NIGEL: Do you mind if I take a look at her.

LUCY: Don't wake her.

NIGEL: I'll listen to her with this. All good. Nothing
to worry about there.

LUCY: Thank you, doctor.

BART: Hi, Nigel.

NIGEL: Bart! I didn't see you there.

BART:	You do good impressions.
NIGEL:	Thanks.
BART:	I saw them kissing, too.
NIGEL:	I thought you were looking round the house. It's a cool house. Better when the sun is shining. It was on the market last year for half a million. We even thought about putting in an offer but then they withdrew it. This used to be the stables. You should see the gardens. And there's a private path that leads down to the sea, the cove. Maybe we can go there after supper when it stops raining.
LUCY:	If it stops raining.
BART:	Lucy says that this one is okay. That that one's yours and that this is Joy's.
NIGEL:	That's Sian's bed.
BART:	I know.
NIGEL:	That's my sister's bed.
BART:	I'm sorry.

A pile of four folded towels fall from the sky.

| LUCY: | They've found the towels. |

BART, LUCY and NIGEL all take a towel back to their beds. The fourth towel remains on the floor. BART lies back down on his bed.

NIGEL:	What time's supper?
LUCY:	You had a McDonald's.
NIGEL:	Who told you?

LUCY points at BART.

	So?
	Maddie's cooking pasta bake.
LUCY:	Is Maddie here?
NIGEL:	She was here first.
LUCY:	I didn't see the car
NIGEL:	They came on the train. Maddie can't drive any more. It's the drugs or something.
LUCY:	I thought she was getting better.
NIGEL:	They're just telling her that to cheer her up.
LUCY:	You mean she's –
NIGEL:	Definintely.
LUCY:	When?
NIGEL:	Any time now.
LUCY:	That's terrible.
NIGEL:	All her hair has fallen out.
LUCY:	Poor Joy. Is there anything you can do?
NIGEL:	I'm not that kind of doctor.
LUCY:	But if she gets really sick.
NIGEL:	I can listen to her with this. (*The stethoscope.*)

NIGEL starts to unpack.

LUCY:	Where *is* Joy, then?
NIGEL:	I thought she was in here.

LUCY:	Jen says she's really struggling – not leaving her room, not speaking to anyone, not eating.
NIGEL:	We're going to have a brilliant holiday, aren't we, a week of this, no Sian.
LUCY:	No Fran.
NIGEL:	And the weather.
LUCY:	*We'll* have a good time though, won't we, me and you?
BART:	It's not heavy metal.

Unpacking.

NIGEL:	What's Sandy doing in here?
LUCY:	She doesn't seem to like me anymore.
NIGEL:	She's muddy.
LUCY:	She's not allowed on the beds.
NIGEL:	She's not allowed in the *house.*
LUCY:	We could bath her.

SANDY presses a button.

Black out. Sound of rain.

Lights up.

JOY is aiming a toy gun at NIGEL and LUCY who are lying spread-eagled on the floor.

NIGEL:	Look, Joy, it's not like that. I didn't mean it like that. When I said she was going to

die I didn't mean she was actually going to die. She's going to be fine. Fine. I'm a doctor. They're really good at this stuff now. Everyone gets ill and then they get better.

LUCY: It was just Nigel being his stupid self, wasn't it, Nigel?

NIGEL: I see this all the time at my surgery.

LUCY: You know what Nigel's like, don't you, silly old Nigel, stupid Nigel –

NIGEL: Alright.

LUCY: *(Struggling to get up.)* JEN. JEN. JOY'S GOT A GUN. SHE'S GOT A –

JOY restrains LUCY.

JOY: Flipping weirdo am I?

LUCY: I didn't know you were there, hiding, which is a bit of a flipping weird thing to do if you ask me. Don't shoot me, don't shoot me.

NIGEL: You should never point that at anyone. Seriously, Joy. Is it loaded?

BART: Hi, Joy. I'm Bart. I'm here with Liesbeth. She and Steve are together now, you heard about that? Fran and Steve split up. That's why Sian's not here.

Look.

You don't know me and I don't know you, but we're about to spend a week together and this is not a particularly great start.

JOY: You know he's not a real doctor.

BART: No, of course not. So he doesn't know what he's talking about, does he.

NIGEL: Actually, I am a real doctor.

BART: Nigel.

NIGEL: I'm just saying.

BART: Joy – I heard you're having a rough time at the moment and I'm really sorry. I know what it feels like.

JOY: No you don't.

LUCY: He does, actually.

(She struggles again.) PAUL. PAUL. HELP ME.

JOY: Poor little Lucy, can't handle it on her own. *(JOY straddles LUCY.)* Tell them it's nothing. Go on. Tell them to keep out of it or I will shoot you, I swear.

They listen.

LUCY: It's all right. IT'S OKAY. IT'S NOTHING, PAUL. WE'RE JUST PLAYING. You're hurting me.

BART: Joy. Why don't you put the gun down?

LUCY: Yeah, put the gun down, Joy, step away from the gun.

JOY: Why should I?

LUCY: Because this is a holiday, Joy. We are here on holiday. And holidays are meant to be fun. We're here to have fun. Remember fun?

JOY: No.

LUCY: Oh, flipping hell, Joy. Never was a person more inaccurately named.

JOY shoots NIGEL.

NIGEL: Ow.

BART hands JOY the last remaining towel.

BART: Would you like a drink or something? Lucy has Ribena.

JOY: I hate Ribena.

JOY hands BART the gun.

BART: I'm going to have a look round the house. Anyone want to come with me?

BART exits.

JOY: It's applecottage18 all lower case. 17 was last year. 2017.

LUCY: Who changes their password every year?

JOY: Who calls their parents by their first name?

LUCY: Who is a baby?

JOY: Who *has* a baby?

LUCY: Me.

JOY: Really?

LUCY: Yes.

JOY: Then shouldn't you look after it?

LUCY: I am looking after it.

JOY: Really?

LUCY: Yes.

JOY: Then where is it?

LUCY: In its pram.

JOY: Really?

LUCY: Yes.

JOY: Sure?

LUCY: Yes.

JOY: Wanna bet?

JOY goes to the pram, whips Jasmine out and throws her to NIGEL.

LUCY: Give her back!

A game of piggy in the middle.

                        My baby! My baby! Give her back!
                        Call the police. PAUL.
                        I'm going to get you, I'm going to kill you,
                        Joy.
                        Nigel, help me.

SANDY is involved now.

                        Sandy, get out of the way. OUT OF THE
                        WAY.
                        You're a freak, Joy. A flipping freak. It's my
                        baby. MY BABY.
                        Sandy. SANDY. Drop it. You'll hurt it. Drop
                        it. SANDY.

SANDY puts the doll down on the floor.

LUCY hits SANDY.

JOY: Pick on someone your own size.

SANDY returns to her control desk.

BART returns.

BART:	Supper's ready.

Lights out. Sound of rain.

Lights up.

The four are on their beds.

JOY is making a paper people-chain.

NIGEL is slowly getting changed into his night clothes – clumsily, under a towel.

BART is reading a foreign graphic novel.

LUCY is attending to her phone and rocking Jasmine.

BART is dressed in onesie pyjamas.

SANDY passes among the beds – being scratched and petted. She spends most of her time with JOY.

NIGEL:	There's always Monkey World.
LUCY:	Over my dead body.
NIGEL:	Or the Donkey Sanctuary.
BART:	But we don't go if it's raining?
NIGEL:	If it's raining, the monkeys, like any sensible primate, stay indoors.
BART:	And the donkeys?
NIGEL:	Walking around in the rain looking at wet donkeys? I can hardly contain myself.
JOY:	The monkeys the dunkeys the monkeys the dunkeys the monkeys the dunkeys the monkeys.
BART:	It's only water.

NIGEL:	What?
BART:	Rain is only water.
NIGEL:	Oh my god. The master has spoken. It's water! Rain is water! Who knew? News flash. 'Rain identified as water by Dutch man –'
JOY:	Leave him alone.
BART:	It's only because Sian's not here and it's not my fault. I am not responsible for the break-up of your family, Nigel. I didn't ask to live in your house. I didn't ask to come here. None of us want to be here anyway.
LUCY:	Jasmine does.

LUCY picks Jasmine out of the pram and holds her.

NIGEL settles down on the bed and takes up his knitting. He is halfway through knitting an animal hat.

NIGEL:	The wind's picking up.
LUCY:	We have no say in what we do anyway.
NIGEL:	They just want to sit around and drink and smoke and talk.
LUCY:	They were steaming through it tonight.
NIGEL:	Even Jen.
LUCY:	Mostly Jen.
NIGEL:	It's like they come here and turn into teenagers.
LUCY:	I'm sorry about Jen.
NIGEL:	At least we now know everything there is to know about cross-pollination.

BART:	It made me very cross.
NIGEL:	What?
BART:	Cross. Cross-pollination. It's a joke. It made me cross. Cross and cross.
LUCY:	Must be a Dutch thing. Steve and Liesbeth were holding hands under the table. Did you see that, Nigel?
NIGEL:	And what was she wearing? We're miles from nowhere and she's dressed like she's going to a nightclub.
BART:	She likes to dress up, that's all.
NIGEL:	Very European.
LUCY:	Paul says Liesbeth 'puts it out'.
BART:	What does that mean?
LUCY:	You know.

LUCY 'puts it out'.

NIGEL:	She's attracting a bee.
BART:	What?
NIGEL:	She's like a flower and my dad is the bee. That's why she dresses colourfully. He's attracted to her and he – he wants to pollinate her!
LUCY:	'Pollinate' her!

Much pleasure with the word 'pollinate'.

> Yeah and Fran's petals have started to fade
> and drop off and that's why Steve left her.
> He went to a brighter flower!
>
> I'm sorry, Nigel, I didn't mean it.

A flash of fury from NIGEL.

He attacks LUCY and they fight – intense, silent grappling, wrestling. It's quite shocking for everyone.

As quickly as it started, the fight stops.

JOY: Fran is a beautiful flower.

NIGEL: *(Calling off.)* WE'RE FINE.
                  YEAH.
                  WE WILL.
                  NIGHT.

LUCY: Sandy. To your place, Sandy.

SANDY returns to the control desk.

They all start to get into their beds.

BART: Do they usually come down?

LUCY: Maddie always used to tuck us in, didn't she,
                  Joy?
                  Joy.

JOY opens her chain of paper people.

NIGEL: Who's this? Who's this?

NIGEL does an impression of JEN – mad hair and boobs and wine.

> Here we see the honey bee approaching the
> flower. 'What on god's green earth is going
> on?' You're a flower and you're a flower and
> you're a flower. Look. Look. I'm pollinating
> you. Etc.

LUCY: Don't sting me! Etc.

Laughter.

BART: You should be a comedian, Nigel.

NIGEL: I do drama. Both Siany and me.

LUCY: When a bee stings you, right, when a bee stings you the sting goes into you and it pulls out all the bee's guts. There's a hook on the sting – a barb – so when it goes into you it can't come out – and as the bee tries to fly away it just flies up to bee heaven.

NIGEL puts on an almost completed knitted animal hat.

NIGEL: I had a teacher once who said that the only animals who go to heaven are animals who look you in the eye. Horses and dogs and cats and cows and things like that. Mammals. You ever been looked in the eye by a bee?

               Sandy will go to heaven, won't you Sandy.

LUCY: Some lizards look you in the eye.

NIGEL: You just think they do.

               Joy never looks you in the eye!

BART: Your teacher was a numpty.

JOY is crying.

               It was a good pasta bake, Joy.

LUCY: Yeah, Joy. It was brilliant.

               Maddie's looking really well.

NIGEL: Yeah, yeah. She looks good without hair.

LUCY: You wouldn't know, even, with that thing on
               her head, the scarf thing.

NIGEL: Yeah, yeah. She looks great with the scarf
               thing.

JOY: Shut up shut up shut up shut up shut up shut
               up shut up shut up.

They settle down to sleep. They sleep.

SANDY performs a yoga sequence and then returns to her control desk.

Black out.

Lights up.

Next day. All in their night clothes.

A hurricane is happening outside. The sound of wind and torrential rain.

The four are all standing on their beds, looking out of the window, listening.

Standing in front of each of them is a child – aged around nine – the same genders, wearing subtly similar clothes. CHILD NIGEL is in a doctor's coat with a stethoscope. CHILD LUCY is holding Jasmine. CHILD JOY is holding the toy gun.

The wind roars.

Black out.

Lights up.

The four adults are sitting on their beds, bored. The four children are running around – playing tag. SANDY is joining in. Rain. More rain.

Black out.

Lights up. Steady rain. Night time.

JOY, BART, LUCY and SANDY are standing around NIGEL's bed. NIGEL is tossing and turning and calling out.

CHILD NIGEL is standing at the head of the bed, also watching.

It's disturbing to watch. The other three look on as he thrashes around.

NIGEL:	NO!
LUCY:	Nigel.
NIGEL:	No, you can't!
LUCY:	Nigel. Shut up.
NIGEL:	She hasn't got any, did you hear me, these are the last and they're mine. They're mine.
LUCY:	Wake up.
NIGEL:	I'm telling you, no. Leave her alone.
BART:	WAKE UP, NIGEL.
NIGEL:	NO. Argh. Keep back! I'll kill you, you bastards.
LUCY:	NIGEL.
NIGEL:	What is it?
BART:	You're shouting.
NIGEL:	What, what? Get them off me. Get them off me.
LUCY:	Nigel, you've woken us all up.
BART:	You're dreaming.
NIGEL:	It's over. It's all over.
BART:	It's a dream.

NIGEL:	There's nothing left. Nothing. NO.

NIGEL becomes conscious of the other three.

BART:	Nigel, you've been having a dream.
LUCY:	We were watching you.
NIGEL:	Everything was falling.
BART:	Look, it's fine. Nothing's fallen. Look.
NIGEL:	What time is it?
LUCY:	Nearly midnight.
NIGEL:	There was a swarm of them.
LUCY:	Of what?
NIGEL:	You know.
LUCY:	No.
NIGEL:	You know!
BART:	Bees?
NIGEL:	No. NO. The bees are all dead. They couldn't dance and now they're dead and everything is falling.
BART:	Wasps?
NIGEL:	NO. NO. We were all – You know. All of us. I really want – I really –
BART:	What?
LUCY:	Do you want me to get Steve?
NIGEL:	Yes – No.
BART:	They're still up. You can hear them in the kitchen.

28

NIGEL:	I didn't want to go there. The world was ending, do you understand?
LUCY:	You're okay, Nigel. The world is still here.
NIGEL:	I didn't want – *(NIGEL starts to cry.)*
JOY:	Nigel.
LUCY:	It was just a stupid dream, Nigel. It's the middle of the night. It was a dream. We all have them.

NIGEL is a bit inconsolable.

CHILD NIGEL slowly leaves.

	Can you shut up so we can all go back to sleep.
NIGEL:	I wish Sian was here.
LUCY:	So do we all, Nigel, blimey, Nigel just shut up. It's a wonder you haven't woken Jasmine.
BART:	Lucy.
LUCY:	Numpty.
	(Calling off.) Steve. STEVE. Nigel's had a nightmare. A nightmare. What? Come down. WHAT? COME DOWN.

LUCY goes upstage.

| | But she's not allowed. SHE'S NOT ALLOWED. |

LUCY returns.

| | He says we're old enough to look after ourselves and that Sandy can be on your bed. Up you go, Sandy. |

SANDY goes onto NIGEL's bed.

> Now can we please all just shut up and try and get some sleep.

The four go back to their beds.

Sound of wind and rain.

JOY:	Nigel.
LUCY:	What?
JOY:	I said 'Nigel'.
NIGEL:	What is it, Joy?
JOY:	Are you okay?
NIGEL:	I thought I was dying.
JOY:	Nigel.
NIGEL:	What?
JOY:	In your dream.
NIGEL:	Yes.
JOY:	You said the bees were all dead.
NIGEL:	They couldn't dance and that's why the world was ending.
BART:	That dream wasn't about bees.
NIGEL:	Yes it was.
BART:	The bees mean something else.
JOY:	Nigel.
LUCY:	Oh, for heaven's sake.
JOY:	In your sleep –

NIGEL: What?

JOY: In your sleep, yeah.
                You said 'bastards'.

The lights dim.

Ballet music.

As the adult actors sleep, CHILD LUCY enters.

Adult LUCY sits up on her bed and 'watches' her.

CHILD LUCY does a short proficient ballet dance.

The dance ends.

LUCY goes back to sleep.

Black out.

Lights up.

Next day.

NIGEL is wearing a knitted animal hat and a duffel coat. He is applying a bandage to Jasmine.

LUCY calling off – reading from a list.

LUCY: Sugar Puffs, Weetos, squeezy cheese –

NIGEL: Not with chives.

LUCY: – not with chives. Pomegranates, Doritos,
                more Haribo, Heat magazine. Nappies for
                Jasmine and a speargun for Joy.

                She wants a speargun. She says that Maddie
                promised her a speargun. A SPEARGUN.

                Why do you want a speargun, Joy?

JOY: For snorkeling.

LUCY: I don't think we'll be doing much snorkeling
                      this week, Joy, do you?

JOY: Yes.

NIGEL: Have you looked out of the window?

LUCY: *(Calling off.)* FOR SNORKELING.

NIGEL: You'll be able to do some snorkeling in the
                      garden if it carries on like this.

LUCY: *(Calling off.)* Come down here, then. COME
                      DOWN.

                      Oh flipping heck, why do I have to do
                      everything?

LUCY exits.

BART and SANDY perform a sequence of simple acrobatics.

BART: Do you like snorkeling, Joy?

JOY: –

NIGEL: Joy? Bart asked you a question.

JOY: Last summer we saw a basking shark.

BART: Okay.

BART takes a badminton racquet out of his bag.

                      Does anyone fancy a game of badminton?

NIGEL: Too windy.

BART hits a shuttlecock. SANDY retrieves it and returns it to BART.

LUCY enters.

LUCY:	They say they're going to the pub on the way back and are we sure we don't want to go.
NIGEL:	Hm. Tesco and then the pub. Let me think.
LUCY:	It's like we don't exist.
BART:	They have a lot to talk about.
NIGEL:	Maddie's staying, isn't she.
LUCY:	Maddie's spending the day in bed.
NIGEL:	Well then.
LUCY:	*(Calling off.)* WE'LL STAY WITH MADDIE. YEAH. NO.
BART:	How is she, Joy?

A small plastic bag drops from the sky. LUCY goes to investigate it.

NIGEL:	They have a secret supply.
LUCY:	Tangfastics.

LUCY picks up the bag and offers it around.

NIGEL:	We've been abandoned.
LUCY:	Again.
NIGEL:	Twister?
LUCY:	Enough games.
NIGEL:	Naked Twister?
BART:	We could go outside?

NIGEL:	Have you seen outside?
LUCY:	We could dress up Sandy. Like last year. Put on a show for them.
NIGEL:	What do you want to do, Joy? Anything you want. You say. We can do anything. Run around with our pants on our heads.
BART:	We could do karaoke?
LUCY:	We don't really do karaoke in this country anymore, Bart.

The sound of car doors closing and a car driving off.

They listen.

JOY:	Draw the curtains and switch out the lights.

Black out.

Lights up dim.

JOY is lying on the floor, rigid.

LUCY:	You're not tense enough, Joy.
JOY:	I am.
NIGEL:	You have to be stiff, Joy, really stiff. Like this.
JOY:	I AM BEING.
LUCY:	No you're not. Like this.

LUCY and NIGEL demonstrate.

	Just really tense everything up.
JOY:	I am I told you. I AM I AM I AM.

LUCY:	All right, Joy, all right.
NIGEL:	Bart – come and help us.
BART:	I don't think it's a good idea.
LUCY:	Come on.
BART:	Think about it.
LUCY:	It's Joy's idea.
NIGEL:	It might be the only idea we get from Joy all week.
BART:	It doesn't feel right.
NIGEL:	Joy?
JOY:	I WANT TO DO IT.
LUCY:	Come on, then.
NIGEL:	We need someone at the head.
BART:	Joy, are you sure?
JOY:	What have I been saying the last five minutes what have I been saying?
NIGEL:	Bart?
BART:	Just once, then.

BART kneels down at JOY's head.

JOY:	Do the face.

The three of them put their hands over JOY's face – and then they each place two fingers under her body.

JOY:	I'm ill.
LUCY:	We say that.

JOY:	Nigel say it. He's the doctor.
NIGEL:	I'm very sorry to say that this patient is tremendously ill.
LUCY/BART:	She's ill?
NIGEL:	Yes, ill.
LUCY/BART:	She's ill.
JOY:	I'm looking worse.
LUCY:	Quiet, Joy.
NIGEL:	Oh dear, oh dear.
LUCY:	What is it, doctor?
NIGEL:	Well, she's definitely looking worse.
LUCY/BART:	She's looking worse?
NIGEL:	She's looking worse.
LUCY/BART:	She's looking worse.
JOY:	I'm dying.
LUCY:	Joy!
NIGEL:	It looks to me like she's dying.
LUCY/BART:	She's dying?
NIGEL:	She's dying.
LUCY/BART:	She's dying.
NIGEL:	Oh, goodness me, she's dead.
LUCY/BART:	She's dead?
NIGEL:	She's dead.
LUCY/BART:	She's dead.

JOY:	NOW. DO IT NOW.
LUCY/NIGEL:	Light as a feather, stiff as a board.
LUCY/NIGEL:	Light as a feather, stiff as a board.
NIGEL:	Bart, you have to join in.
BART:	This is for kids.
LUCY:	Bart!
LUCY/NIGEL/BART:	Light as a feather, stiff as a board.
LUCY/NIGEL/BART:	Light as a feather, stiff as a board. Etc.

They try to lift JOY with two fingers each.

JOY:	Ow.
LUCY:	Concentrate.
LUCY/NIGEL/BART:	Light as a feather, stiff as a board.
LUCY/NIGEL/BART:	Light as a feather, stiff as a board. Etc.

As they chant, the nine-year-old girl from the beginning enters the stage (CHILD JOY). She is focused on JOY. SANDY is able to see the girl.

The adults fail to lift JOY.

The girl approaches JOY.

NIGEL:	It's useless.
JOY:	You were digging into me.
NIGEL:	I was not.
JOY:	You were.
NIGEL:	Bored as a board.

LUCY:	You weren't stiff enough.
JOY:	I was.
LUCY:	Try me.
NIGEL:	If we can't lift Joy then there's no chance with you.
LUCY:	You saying I'm fat?
NIGEL:	No.
LUCY:	I'm not fat, am I, Bart?
BART:	It's not about that.
LUCY:	It's to do with concentration, isn't it, Bart?
BART:	If you want it enough you can lift anything.
LUCY:	Exactly. You can lift like a car or something if you really need to. If someone is stuck under it, like your child or –

JOY sees CHILD JOY and starts to scream.

NIGEL:	What?

CHILD JOY starts to leave – slowly.

NIGEL:	What?
JOY:	I rose up!
LUCY:	What?
JOY:	I rose up. I rose up. I rose up.
NIGEL:	Joy?
JOY:	I started to lift up!
NIGEL:	You didn't.

JOY:	I did.
LUCY:	Really?
JOY:	I did I did!
NIGEL:	Oh, for god's sake, Joy.

CHILD JOY exits.

JOY screams again.

JOY:	There, look, look, a shadow!
LUCY:	Joy.
JOY:	There! Look!
LUCY:	Where?
JOY:	There. I could feel it, just lifting me up.
NIGEL:	Maybe it was Sandy.
JOY:	It was a shadow. You don't believe me. It's true. I was floating.
NIGEL:	No one touched you.
JOY:	It was an invisible hand. It was something like a ghost or a spirit. I saw something. I saw something. You saw it, didn't you, Bart, you saw it.
BART:	I'm sure you felt / something.
JOY:	It was real. It was a ghost or God.
LUCY:	Do you want me to get Maddie, Joy?
BART:	Leave it.
NIGEL:	*(Calling off.)* MADDIE.

JOY:	It touched me and lifted me up. You don't know. No one knows.
LUCY:	Are you okay, Joy?
NIGEL:	Calm down, Joy.
JOY:	It was a ghost. A ghost.
NIGEL:	*(Calling off.)* NO. SHE'S OKAY. IT'S NOTHING.
JOY:	You don't know because you don't care. None of you. I hate this place. I hate it. I hate it.

JOY is in tears.

SANDY moves between the four of them – jumping at them, hugging them, holding them, licking them.

LUCY:	SANDY!

SANDY retreats.

JOY:	You don't understand.
LUCY:	THEN YOU SHOULD EXPLAIN IT TO US, SHOULDN'T YOU.

JOY exits.

BART:	What did we do?
NIGEL:	We didn't do anything.
BART:	We encouraged her!
LUCY:	It was her idea.
BART:	It was a bad idea.
NIGEL:	How were we meant to know that?
BART:	Her mum is ill.

NIGEL:	That's just Joy. It's what she's like.
LUCY:	You don't know her.
BART:	I've been with her for three days now, I've got a pretty good idea.
NIGEL:	Well, I've known her for nine sodding years and she's always been like that.
BART:	And that's okay, is it? Because she's always been like that it's okay for her to be like that?
NIGEL:	I don't bloody know.
BART:	She's your friend.
NIGEL:	She hasn't got any friends.
BART:	Nigel.
LUCY:	How can you be friends with a freak? Seriously, how? You try and have a conversation and she doesn't say anything and then when she does say something it's like that.
BART:	Maybe she's unwell.
NIGEL:	She's sick in the head.
LUCY:	It's her mum who's sick; there's nothing wrong with Joy.
BART:	Exactly, think how you would feel if your mum was sick.
NIGEL:	My mum isn't even here.
BART:	But she's not ill, is she?
NIGEL:	She's worse than ill, she's not here. I'd settle for an ill mum if she were here at least.

BART:	None of them are here. / Look.
NIGEL:	And do you know the reason why my mum is not here?
BART:	Don't start, / Nigel.
NIGEL:	Because your mum couldn't keep her dirty hands off my dad.
BART:	You say one more word about that –
NIGEL:	What? What? Yeah? Yeah?

A stand off.

LUCY:	Maddie hasn't always been ill but Joy has always been a freak.
BART:	We should do something. All together. A project.
LUCY:	It's still raining.
BART:	Indoors. Make her feel wanted.
LUCY:	What?
BART:	I don't know. Make something. Maybe put on a show, like Lucy said. Build something. Do something.
LUCY:	I could dance for her.
BART:	Together, I mean, Lucy – with Joy.
NIGEL:	I don't think she would be in to that.
BART:	How do you know?
LUCY:	Go after her, Nigel.
NIGEL:	You go.
LUCY:	No, you.

NIGEL: Why me?

LUCY: She might do herself a mischief.

NIGEL: Well?

LUCY: You're a doctor.

NIGEL: Oh, for pity's sake.

NIGEL goes after her.

BART: Where's Joy's dad?

LUCY: A one night stand, Maddie said.

BART: No wonder she sees ghosts.

LUCY: Do you see ghosts, Bartolomeüs?

BART: I sometimes think I see my dad. Out of the
                corner of my eyes, you know. And then my
                heart jumps and I think he is back again. But
                then I know it's not him and it's like I lose
                him all over again. But I like seeing him. I
                like to remember what he looks like. My
                mum says I look like him. That makes me
                feel good, you know. Like he is in me. Like
                he is part of me.

LUCY: What was your dad's name?

BART: Adrian.

LUCY: Did he lose his hair – like Maddie?

BART: He didn't have much hair to start with.

LUCY: I hope I never look like *my* dad.

BART: I can't see you with a beard.

LUCY: I do look like my mum, though. I have her
                hair.

BART:	You have nice hair.
LUCY:	Thanks.
BART:	I didn't mean it like that. Just – Can we shut up about hair?
LUCY:	You seen the way your mum and Steve can't take their hands off each other.
BART:	None of them seem to take much notice of us here.
LUCY:	They think we can look after ourselves.
BART:	Can't we?
LUCY:	Can we? We're too young to look after ourselves.
BART:	You think?
LUCY:	They say it's a holiday like it's a holiday from us. Maddie was always the one who spent time with us. She was always the fun one. And Fran. We would have been having a great time if it weren't for –
BART:	We have to make our own entertainment.
LUCY:	With you.
BART:	You should talk to Joy.
LUCY:	Nigel's gone.
BART:	Another girl, I mean.
LUCY:	Can't believe you and Nigel are the same age. You're so much more mature.
BART:	You should go.
LUCY:	Bart. I wanted to say something to you.

44

BART: What?

LUCY: It won't rain for ever.

A moment. LUCY does a little dance. She kisses BART on the cheek.

LUCY exits.

BART: Nog vier dagen.
                      Verlos me uit mijn lijden.
                      Prik me lek, schiet me dood.
                      Steek het in je reet, Sandy. *

                      (*Another four days…
                      Take me out of my misery.
                      Punch a hole in me, shoot me.
                      Stick it up your ass, Sandy.)

SANDY: I snap at flies in the air.

A sound is heard. The lights flicker.

BART looks at SANDY. SANDY looks at BART.

A ten-year-old boy has entered (CHILD BART). BART and the boy look at each other. SANDY leaps and jumps around the ten-year-old boy.

CHILD BART hands a microphone to BART. BART hands a microphone to CHILD BART. CHILD BART switches on the karaoke machine.

A song starts to play – not heavy metal but something fairly indie.

BART and CHILD BART start to sing together.

JOY enters. She stands and watches. With her is CHILD JOY.

BART hands his microphone to JOY and CHILD JOY. They start to sing. They can really sing. LUCY enters and watches. Alongside her is CHILD LUCY.

The music increases in volume and intensity.

LUCY and CHILD LUCY dance.

The music fills the theatre.

NIGEL enters.

NIGEL: Quiet.
You have to be quiet.
Bloody quiet.
All of you be QUIET.

NIGEL switches off the karaoke machine. Silence.

NIGEL: Didn't you hear me?
Maddie's trying to sleep.

JOY attacks NIGEL.

The sound of howling wind and rain. The children disappear.

JOY: You're lying, you liar. You liar. She's nothing to do with you. She wouldn't say that. She loves music. She loves to hear it. You know that, Nigel. She wants us to sing. She's the best dancer. She's the best. It's not her fault. She'll get better and then she'll show you. So shut up, Nigel. Shut up shut up shut up.

The fight subsides.

Silence.

Sandy. Put the music on. Put it on. PUT IT ON, SANDY.

The music starts again – super loud. Super heavy metal.

The days passing.

An intermingling of adult actors and children. Becoming increasingly freer. The stage becoming increasingly cluttered.

All of them in waterproof ponchos – including SANDY.

Black out.

Music stops – silence. All four are wearing knitted novelty animal hats. All four are lying on their bellies on their beds.

LUCY is reading to them from her mum's book about bees. Everyone is bored.

LUCY: Bees depend on their habitat for nutrition, and when an ecosystem decays, bee health declines in parallel, leaving bees more susceptible to other threats such as -

Black out.

Music again.

An indoor game of badminton.

CHILD NIGEL is playing BART.

Pillows drop from the sky. A pillow fight among adults and children.

Black out.

Music again.

A game of dressing up. Each dressed outlandishly in blankets and rugs and adult clothing.

Towards the end, a blue light starts flashing.

Black out.

Music stops.

Lights up.

The blue flashing light is still visible.

CHILD JOY is present on stage.

NIGEL and BART. On their respective beds.

They are still in their makeshift costumes.

NIGEL is still in his animal hat and is applying make-up to himself.

BART has a towel wrapped round his head like a turban.

SANDY also has a hat on her head.

NIGEL: You either have it or you don't. And if you
don't have it then you're never going to get
it. Even if you practice and practice you're
never going to get it. It's a special talent,
Bart. It's not a thing you can learn. That's
what all the great actors have. Sian and I go
to a drama club. So, like for Joy, she's not
someone who you would naturally say 'has
it'. And that means that she probably never
will 'have it' even if she did loads and loads
of classes. Now you can blub about it or you
can think about what you *do* have and do
that instead. So, maybe Joy is good at maths,
maybe. Or looking after animals. She will
have other talents and maybe she hasn't
found out what they are yet. I mean I have
other talents like being a doctor and helping
people and making things like this hat. But
also I can make people laugh and be an
actor. You're good with the music. Lucy can
dance and is a very good mother. Being a
good mother is not something that everyone
can do. Some mothers only think about
themselves or put their own things first. Not
looking in any direction in particular, Bart.

LUCY enters, still wearing improvised dressing up clothes, carrying Jasmine.

LUCY: They're not taking her to hospital.

BART: Why not?

LUCY: She wanted to stay here. So they've put her
on her drugs here, in her room. She's on a
sort of drip thing.

BART:	Does it mean she's –
LUCY:	They think she's okay. It's just the drugs make her poorly.
BART:	Where's Joy?
LUCY:	With her.
BART:	Where's everyone else?
LUCY:	Paul and Jen have gone for a walk.
NIGEL:	In the rain?
LUCY:	It's only water. Liesbeth and your dad are in the kitchen with the doctor.
BART:	Why don't they come and tell us?
LUCY:	Everyone's upset.
BART:	Do you know what's happening, Nigel?
NIGEL:	Not really.
BART:	Have you seen her?
NIGEL:	I don't really, you know – It's not – There isn't a Fisher Price chemotherapy set.
LUCY:	They always keep us in the dark.
BART:	I'm surprised that no one has taken the time to tell us – all this holiday – to tell us what's going on.
LUCY:	They've got a lot on their plates.
NIGEL:	And the weather –
BART:	Are we still going to do the show?
NIGEL:	The show must go on!

BART:	It's a nice way to end the holiday for everyone, I suppose.
LUCY:	This has been the worst holiday I have ever had.
NIGEL:	Maybe, as we get older, holidays will just get worse and worse.
BART:	Until we can have holidays on our own.

The sound of a vehicle leaving. The flashing blue light stops.

CHILD JOY 'enters' the scene. (There are now three adults and one child.)

SANDY goes to her and they hug.

NIGEL:	Hi, Joy.
LUCY:	Anything we can get you, Joy? A Ribena?
BART:	She hates Ribena.
NIGEL:	Are you all right to carry on rehearsing, Joy?
LUCY:	If you want to have a rest, we can leave you alone and you can just lie down.
	So, we'll take it really gently, okay. Nigel?
NIGEL:	Yes. Yes. I was just saying to Bart that, Joy, you know, you don't need to do everything. Not everyone can do everything. So you can just take a back seat and we'll – you know – You can help me with the costumes if you like. That's just as important as the acting. Here.

NIGEL goes to his doctor's case.

	This will help you.

He gives CHILD JOY a Tic Tac.

LUCY: So the story so far.

NIGEL: Yes.

         So, Sandy and Jasmine are getting married,
         is that right?

LUCY: That's right.

NIGEL: But on the night of their wedding they are
         kidnapped.

LUCY: Not kidnapped, but – captured. Imprisoned.
         Imprisoned by a foreign prince. Bart, you're
         the prince. An Arab prince, Bart, with that
         thing on your head. And the only way the
         prince will release Sandy and Jasmine is if
         I dance for him. So then the prince puts on
         some music.

NIGEL: Not your weird stuff.

BART: Nigel –

NIGEL: And then you dance.

LUCY: So I do a dance. And the prince can sing – if
         you have to, Bart. And then the prince falls
         in love with me and releases his prisoners.
         We'll probably have to kiss. And so there
         are two weddings – me and the prince and
         Sandy and Jasmine.

         There.

NIGEL: And what am I?

LUCY: You're the storyteller to introduce it. And
         you can be the prince's doctor if you want.

NIGEL: What does he do?

LUCY: He can marry us.

BART:	And that's it?
NIGEL:	There'll be other things.
BART:	What.
NIGEL:	You know.
LUCY:	We can dress Sandy up.
BART:	Well it sounds great.
NIGEL:	Thanks.
LUCY:	He's being sarcastic.
NIGEL:	Well what do you suggest?
BART:	I thought Joy was going to do something. I thought that was the idea.
LUCY:	You can't make Joy do something if she doesn't want to.
NIGEL:	Do you want to do something, Joy? See?
BART:	I'm out.
LUCY:	What?
BART:	This is / not –
LUCY:	Joy could be the prison guard?
BART:	Princes and weddings?
LUCY:	It's what the public wants.
BART:	Don't you think we're a little old for all that?
LUCY:	It's not easy putting on a show, Bart.
NIGEL:	Right.

LUCY: You have to think about your audience.
           They want to be entertained, Bart. It's not
           all about being serious. That's why they're
           called 'plays'. Maddie would want to see
           something to make her happy. Her life is
           hard enough – nothing personal, Joy. This
           is a chance to show the grown-ups what we
           can do and cheer everyone up.

NIGEL: Joy – do you want to do a show tomorrow?
           For the grown-ups? Yes or no?

CHILD JOY: Yes.

Sound of rain.

Scenes of preparation.

The beds are placed in new positions.

SANDY is dressed up.

Costumes evolve.

The lights are adjusted.

Sound levels of the karaoke machine are set.

A vocal warm up. A physical limber, etc.

BART is replaced by CHILD BART.

Two adults now, and two children.

NIGEL: And Paul and Jenny can sit there. Dad and
           Liesbeth there. Maddie there. And Jasmine
           can sit here. Next to Sandy.

LUCY: And then when they come in, you can
           be here, Joy. Go there. Stand there. And
           then, Nigel, you come in and you start with
           something like, like, 'Ladies and gentlemen',
           and then you start the story and we come in.
           Is everyone ready?

NIGEL: Bart, can we have some music playing – for when they come in? Something nice.

CHILD BART starts some music playing from the karaoke machine.

LUCY: Okay. Okay. Let's go and get them.

          (Calling off.) OKAY. We're ready! You can come down now. PAUL – you can bring everyone down now. MUM.

          MUM. JEN.

NIGEL: DAD. It's going to start.

          Lucy – go and get them.

LUCY: You go.

NIGEL: No, you.

LUCY exits.

They wait.

NIGEL: We should have made some tickets! And popcorn!

CHILD LUCY enters.

NIGEL: Where are they?

CHILD LUCY: They've gone to the pub.

NIGEL: What?

CHILD LUCY: The pub. They've walked to the pub.

NIGEL: But we told them it was on.

CHILD LUCY: They forgot.

NIGEL: Did Maddie go?

CHILD LUCY: She's coming down.

54

| NIGEL: | I can't believe this. They knew we were doing this. They knew how hard we've worked. Stupid bloody waste of space. I give up. I bloody give up trying. Rubbish. Bloody rubbish. |

NIGEL storms off.

SANDY goes off after him.

Three children onstage – no adults for the first time.

CHILD BART turns off the music.

Into this moment enters MADDIE (down through the audience.).

MADDIE is played by the actor who played adult JOY.

She looks frail and vulnerable, wearing a head scarf.

She walks with a stick.

MADDIE:	Where do you want me?
CHILD JOY:	Everyone else has gone to the pub.
MADDIE:	They don't know what they're missing.
CHILD LUCY:	We can't do the show.
MADDIE:	Why not?
CHILD LUCY:	Because they've gone.
MADDIE:	I'm here.
CHILD LUCY:	We can't just do it for you, Maddie.
MADDIE:	Why not?
CHILD LUCY:	Because that wasn't the plan. That wasn't the plan. We're doing it for the grown-ups.
MADDIE:	You can do it for yourselves!

CHILD LUCY:	No. Not just – I can't believe they forgot.
MADDIE:	They didn't realise it was so important, Lucy.
CHILD LUCY:	Well it IS! It really IS.
MADDIE:	You could do it later.
CHILD LUCY:	We were ready to do it NOW.
MADDIE:	Shall I go back up?
CHILD BART:	We'll do it now.
CHILD LUCY:	Bart!
CHILD BART:	It's their fault if they miss it, isn't it, Joy?
CHILD JOY:	It can be for us.
CHILD LUCY:	No it can't.
CHILD JOY:	You can sit here, mum.

MADDIE sits at the front of the audience. CHILD JOY sits beside her.

MADDIE:	How exciting! A show just for me! I feel like the Queen of Sheeba.
CHILD BART:	Are you feeling alright, Maddie?
MADDIE:	I'm feeling fine, thank you, Bart.
CHILD LUCY:	We need Nigel. Nigel is the story teller. We can't do it without Nigel.
	(Calling off.) NIGEL!

CHILD NIGEL and SANDY enter. SANDY is dressed up outrageously. CHILD NIGEL is dressed normally. He takes centre stage.

CHILD LUCY:	Where's your costume, Nigel?
CHILD NIGEL:	This is stupid. There's no bloody point in it.

CHILD LUCY:	Nigel!
CHILD BART:	Go on, Nigel. You'll be great.
MADDIE:	Come on, Nigel. I'm looking forward to it!
CHILD NIGEL:	Once upon a time – Once upon a time there was a dog called Sandy who was in love with a princess called Jasmine. Sandy – come and stand here. Sandy!

SANDY runs around the stage. Things fall apart.

	Oh, I give up. I'm not doing this. Forget it.
CHILD LUCY:	Nigel's right. This is stupid. Bloody stupid.
CHILD NIGEL:	Forget it. Just forget it.

CHILD NIGEL and CHILD LUCY storm off.

SANDY is on the stage with CHILD BART.

SANDY looks at CHILD BART. She looks at MADDIE.

SANDY starts to speak.

As she speaks, the stage starts to come alive.

SANDY:	You other smells. You others. You big shapes, you, I snap. Here is the. Here is the. SIT.

SANDY runs round.

	Here, good here-here good-here. Here is the play-play-play. The small shapes have worked, sad shapes have, have made. You curl circle down. Lick bee snap. Bee snap-snap.

SANDY runs around again. Starts again.

Sitting still. STILL. Here's a tale-tail in a sniff-sniff. Wags and. Wag-wag. You people, you. You big shapes who. You now; you now-now. Hey girl. This bit. This bit is GREAT! IT'S THE GREATEST BIT. Hold it in. HOLD IT. Round and round and round. Sniff-sniffs, wet snout out, snout shout out. No danger. No dying-danger here. Not here. In. This. Play. Here, girl. Rain falls. Snap drops. Shout! Wet stop. Sniff stop. Stone stop. Lamp stop. Ball stop. Ball ball stop. Stop-bum. Turn round, bum sniff. LADIES AND GENTLEMEN BUM SNIFF. BISCUIT! Oh, that's all very squirrel, all very fly, all very sound of, sound of – listen. Smell to your anticipation. Hear to your EXPECTATION. Smell your inside sounds. Hear your inside smells. There's play, there's play – You things! You things over, you! You over in the other colour, in the other sound, the other sound wave, wave, other over, see other over, you you you. Tail down. You tale down.

Woof rough it is. That's rough. The world this is. The world that is us.

Sit. Stand. Sit. Wait. Wait. Wait. Play. Play. Here's it. Here. Is. The. Play.

Silence.

SANDY looks around. She looks at CHILD JOY. She looks at CHILD BART.

SANDY exits.

CHILD BART goes to the karaoke machine and presses play. Huge music starts to play from every inch of the theatre. The lights change.

CHILD JOY picks up one of the karaoke microphones. Her voice fills the theatre.

CHILD JOY: This is where our story starts.
               Our story starts here.

CHILD BART takes up the second microphone.

CHILD BART: Here on this island.

CHILD JOY: This island full of ghosts.

CHILD BART: Here where the summers are hot and the
               towels are always there when they say they'll
               be.

CHILD JOY: And there's always milk in the fridge.

CHILD BART: Here on this island.

CHILD JOY: Where death never visits.

CHILD BART: This Canary Island. Full of the most
               beautiful –

CHILD JOY: – bees.

CHILD BART: The most beautiful bees you have ever
               imagined.
               The sound of beautiful buzzing.

CHILD JOY: Bees of every colour and size and shape
               you ever saw. Bees that never sting you so
               they live forever. Bees as big as birds that fly
               together –

CHILD BART: In flocks.

CHILD JOY: Flocks of bees across the island skies.
               An iridescent flock of bees fly slowly across
               the stage.
               And when the bees fly overhead, when they
               do that, the cars slow down and the babies
               stop crying and the bullies stop bullying.

CHILD BART: And arguments end and sick people get better and everyone listens.

CHILD JOY: They listen to the beautiful buzz.

CHILD BART: Here on this island.

CHILD JOY: This beautiful island.

The stage is filled with beauty. Flowers, lights, colours, sounds.

But then something starts to happen.

CHILD BART: The sky gets darker. In this summer where it never rains, it looks like fog.

CHILD JOY: Or smoke.

CHILD BART: Nobody notices at first.

CHILD JOY: They go about their lives.

CHILD BART: But the sky slowly gets darker and darker.

The music becomes sinister.

The beauty starts to fade.

Smoke begins to fill the air.

And the bees get sick.

CHILD JOY: Their buzz loses its buzz and their wings get weaker and they stop making honey. Their flocks become smaller and the babies keep on crying.

CHILD BART: And the doctors can do nothing about it.

CHILD JOY: And nobody listens anymore.

CHLID BART: And death comes to the island for the first time ever and the flowers start to drop their petals because the bees can't help them anymore.

The bees start to fall from the sky. The flowers start to wilt and fade.

The sound of falling things.

Music.

CHILD BART and CHILD JOY sing a duet.

THE SONG OF CROSS-POLLINATION

The bees know.

In the world
Something is coming
Something is looming
In the sky.

We know.

In ourselves
Something is happening
Something is changing
It won't go.

We know.

The Bee is all
The End is all
The petals fall
We're on our own.

The bees know.

No pollination
From flower to flower to flower to flower
No future
We know.

No future
From adult to child to child to child.
No future
We know.

When I was a child
I thought as a child
But now the adults
Have put away childish things.
Now we are scared.

The stage changes to menace.

CHILD JOY: The first person to spot the problem is a
                      young girl called –

CHILD BART: Sian.

CHILD JOY: Sian is a brilliant, brave young girl.

CHILD NIGEL enters dressed as Sian – with overtones of Liesbeth's 'putting out'.

She can climb up curtains and stays with
her mum and does what she wants because
she is wild and we miss her. Here she is
performed by her brother, Nigel.

Sian is out walking with her dog, Sandy.

CHILD NIGEL: Sandy! Here, girl.

SANDY enters, dressed outrageously.

SANDY: BUM SNIFF EVERYONE!

CHILD JOY: While they are out walking by the cove, they
                      find a fallen bee on the ground and Siany
                      picks it up.

*CHILD NIGEL picks up a bee – a puppet – made from a version of the doll
that is Jasmine.*

CHILD JOY:	The bee looks at Sian and tears roll from its eyes.
CHILD NIGEL:	*(In the microphone.)* Can you say I'm also a doctor?
CHILD BART:	What's wrong, says Sian – who is also a doctor.
CHILD NIGEL:	What's wrong? Why are you crying?
CHILD JOY:	But the bee is too weak to even speak. It looks like it's seen a ghost.
CHILD BART:	Sian says to Sandy, 'We've got to do something.'
CHILD NIGEL:	We've got to do something. Without the bees, everything will die.
CHILD BART:	And Sandy says, 'Yes, we must get help.'
SANDY:	SCRATCHY SCRATCHY SCRATCHY!
CHILD BART:	Says Sandy, who knows just what to do.
SANDY:	BISCUIT BALL BOUNCE!
CHILD JOY:	So Sian, Sandy and the bee go to the adults to get help.
CHILD NIGEL:	But no one knows where the adults have gone!
CHILD BART:	Yes! The adults have gone!
CHILD JOY:	They've disappeared into the smoke – without anyone noticing.
CHILD BART:	Yes.
CHILD JOY:	They were tired darling or when I've finished this or they were at the office or drunk too much or forgotten their keys or

	give me five minutes won't you or NOT NOW.
CHILD NIGEL:	*(To MADDIE.)* Have you seen the adults?
MADDIE:	No!
CHILD NIGEL:	Where have the adults gone?
CHILD BART:	And as they look for the adults, they see that the sky is getting darker and darker.
CHILD JOY:	Smokier and foggier.
CHILD BART:	The only place where there is no smoke is the top of a mountain.
CHILD NIGEL:	The mountain of Honiton!
CHILD BART:	At the top of Honiton mountain lives a professor who was banished from the town many years ago because –
CHILD NIGEL:	Her hair was all wrong.
CHILD JOY:	She is the only adult left.
CHILD BART:	And so Sian and Sandy and the dying bee climb the mountain to see her.

CHILD BART, CHILD JOY and CHILD NIGEL sing.

THE SONG OF THE LONELY SCIENTIST

There comes a time when an adult is needed
It pains me to say it but an adult is needed
To reach the high places. To open stubborn jars.
To explain this law or that conundrum.

The lonely scientist
Sits on a hill

Wondering still
If there's hope
If anyone will listen

Adults we trust you with our future.
Adults we need you to explain
All the things that you have done.
All the ways you've let us down
Help us
Help us

Our world is changing
We need an expert.
So teach us.
Oh, teach us.

As they sing, CHILD LUCY enters. She is dressed like her mother – in her mother's clothes. A jacket much too big for her. Shoes much too big for her. Padded bra. Mad hair. She is surrounded by small bees.

CHILD LUCY does a dance as they sing.

CHILD JOY leaves as the song ends.

CHILD LUCY:	What on god's green earth is going on? I am the Professor. I live on the mountain of Honiton. Look at my hair. Look at my big boobies.
CHILD NIGEL:	Professor, professor. My name is Sian.
CHILD LUCY:	I thought you would never visit me again, Sian. I messaged you.
CHILD NIGEL:	Professor, the bees are dying and all the adults have disappeared for ever. What can we do?
CHILD LUCY:	Let me see your bee.

CHILD LUCY inspects the bee.

	It's just what I thought. I said that this would happen. I even wrote a book about it. But none of you flipping read it. None of you read it and now look what's happening.
CHILD NIGEL:	How can we know what to do without the adults?
CHILD LUCY:	You must trust yourselves.
CHILD NIGEL:	But I am only a young girl.
CHILD LUCY:	Where is the boy called Bart?
CHILD BART:	Here, Professor.
CHILD LUCY:	Come here, boy. You are a wise young man. You have travelled far and seen many things. I will tell you how to save the bees – but first you must kiss me.
CHILD BART:	Do I have to?
CHILD LUCY:	Your kiss will help save the world.
CHILD BART:	I don't really want to.
CHILD LUCY:	All right then. I just thought it would be nice.
CHILD BART:	Maybe in a few years time.
CHILD LUCY:	It's a deal.
CHILD NIGEL:	Come on! We're running out of time!
CHILD LUCY:	Look out for Death.
CHILD NIGEL:	How will we know what Death looks like?
CHILD LUCY:	Sandy will tell you. She will feel her arrival before you do. If you meet her, here, take this Ribena.
CHILD NIGEL:	How will it help?

CHILD LUCY: Death hates Ribena, isn't that right, Maddie?

MADDIE: Yes!

SANDY starts to go crazy. The earth starts to open up. Flashes of light. The beds crack apart.

SANDY: HAIR RAISE HACKLES UP TAIL DOWN.

CHILD NIGEL: What is it, Sandy? What is it, girl?

SANDY: DANGER COMING. DANGER.

There is a huge rumble of thunder and CHILD JOY appears – dressed in a snorkel and goggles and flippers, carrying a speargun. Her voice distorted by the snorkel and amplified by the microphone.

CHILD JOY: I am DEATH. Because you didn't listen, I have taken the bees. And because I have taken the bees the adults have gone. And now I will take you and destroy your island. First I will start with the Professor because she has terrible hair.

CHILD LUCY: It's not my fault. It's genetic.

CHILD JOY and CHILD LUCY fight. It is epic.

The Professor is destroyed.

CHILD LUCY: Argh. I am dead. You must do everything you can to save the world. You are our only hope. All the adults have gone. It's down to you now. You can do it.

The Professor dies.

CHILD JOY: Now it is your turn. I will destroy you like I have destroyed everything. Raaaaah.

CHILD JOY turns on CHILD NIGEL and SANDY.

Another epic fight.

In the end, CHILD NIGEL disables death by squirting her with Ribena – and then the bee stings her – and thereby dies itself. ('Don't sting her, bee, or you will die.')

As Death dies, an adult figure descends from on high.

Huge music.

It is the adult actor who played BART – but now this is ADRIAN, BART's father.

Music and light and joy.

CHILD NIGEL: Who are you?

CHILD BART: I know who that is. His name is Adrian. He's my dad.

CHILD LUCY: But I thought your dad was dead.

CHILD BART: He is.

Hello dad.

ADRIAN: Hello, Bartolomeüs. I just wanted to say good luck. To tell you that you can do it. All of you.

CHILD BART: Thanks, dad.

ADRIAN: You're looking more and more like me.

CHILD BART: Thanks, dad.

ADRIAN: That's not necessarily a good thing.

CHILD BART: I'm sorry mum is dating again.

ADRIAN: That's fine.

CHILD BART: Steve is not as cool as you.

ADRIAN: Don't feel bad about it.

CHILD BART:	I'll try.
ADRIAN:	Look after Liesbeth.
CHILD BART:	I will. I miss you.
ADRIAN:	I miss you.
CHILD BART:	Dad.
ADRIAN:	Yes?
CHILD BART:	The bee died stinging Death to death.
CHILD NIGEL:	It was the last bee, Mr. Bart. It sacrificed its life for us.
ADRIAN:	Don't worry, Sian. Now that Death is dead, the bees will come back, I promise.
CHILD JOY:	Will the adults come back, Mr. Bart?
ADRIAN:	Maybe or maybe not. But it doesn't matter, Joy, because you are the adults now. They are inside you.
CHILD BART:	Come and visit me again, won't you, dad.
ADRIAN:	I'll try. Now celebrate. You have saved the world. That deserves a song and a dance at least. It's a happy ending.

ADRIAN ascends and, as he does so, the dead bee takes flight up into the sky.

Music and song.

THE SONG OF THE HAPPY ENDING.

> It's okay.
> Okay.
> Everything is okay.
> Everything will be just fine.

>   Endings are beginnings
>   Endings are beginnings
>
>   Goodbye here is Hello there
>   Hello somewhere else.
>   Hello!
>
>   It's going to be okay.
>   Whatever happens, it's going to be okay
>   You have the answer
>   You can do it

The stage has completely transformed.

MADDIE gets up and joins in the song and the dance.

SANDY is totally exuberant.

In the midst of the post-show party, JENNY enters. Back from the pub. Played by the adult who played LUCY. Raincoat on. Mad hair.

JENNY: Hey. Hey. Hey.

The music stops.

                    What on god's green earth is going on?

CHILD LUCY runs to her mum.

CHILD LUCY: You missed the play.

JENNY: Are you wearing my bra?

CHILD LUCY: We saved the world and death died and
                    Maddie danced, look! And Sian was here.
                    And Bart's dad came to say goodbye. Isn't
                    that right, Maddie?

MADDIE: It certainly is.

JENNY: Are you sure you should be dancing,
                    Maddie?

MADDIE:	Never felt surer! The children put on a wonderful show. I didn't know they were all so talented. Joy, darling, you were an excellent Death.
CHILD JOY:	Thanks, mum.
CHILD LUCY:	Joy, you were amazing.

STEVE enters – played by the adult actor who played NIGEL.

STEVE:	What's happened here?
CHILD NIGEL:	Dad. We said there was going to be a play. We told you.
STEVE:	Look at this / mess.
CHILD NIGEL:	It was probably the best play that's ever been done and you missed it. YOU MISSED IT. Mum wouldn't have missed it, she wouldn't –
STEVE:	NIGEL!
CHILD NIGEL:	It was better than *Wicked*.
MADDIE:	Don't be upset, Nigel. You can do it again.
CHILD NIGEL:	We can never do it again.
STEVE:	We're leaving first thing in the morning and someone has to clean up this mess, put these beds back how they were.
MADDIE:	I'll help them.
STEVE:	Maddie, you shouldn't be up on your feet.
MADDIE:	I'm feeling a lot better for it, Steve – you missed quite a show.
JENNY:	It sounds like it.

STEVE:	Who's going to clear this up?
MADDIE:	We'll all do it after supper.
JENNY:	You must all be starving.
CHILD BART:	Sorry we made such a mess, Steve.
STEVE:	Well, think about what you're doing next time.
JENNY:	Come upstairs, everyone. We've bought chips. Up you go. Come on. Out.

They all start to exit.

To your place, Sandy.

CHLID JOY is the last on the stage. She hugs SANDY.

| CHILD JOY: | Thanks for saving the world, Sandy. |

CHILD JOY leaves.

SANDY is alone with us.

SANDY:	Real reason. Real run run.
	You human shapes. You. Curl circle down.
	The. Play. They. Made. Is. Over.
	Sleep.

SANDY presses a button.

Black out.

END

www.ingramcontent.com/pod-product-compliance
Ingram Content Group UK Ltd.
Pitfield, Milton Keynes, MK11 3LW, UK
UKHW020725280225
455688UK00012B/508